LIBRARY
MURRAY STATE UNIVERSITY

D1445627

Talking Back

By the same author

Contentions
Kisses
Talking to Bede (with notes)

Verlaine: **Femmes/Hombres: Women/Men** *(translator)*
Heine: **The Lazarus Poems** *(translator)*
Virgil and Dryden: **The Georgics** *(editor)*

Talking Back

Alistair Elliot

DISCARDED

Secker & Warburg
London

PR
6055
L47
T3
1982

First published in England 1982 by
Martin Secker & Warburg Limited
54 Poland Street, London W1V 3DF

Copyright © Alistair Elliot 1982

British Library Cataloguing in Publication Data

Elliot, Alistair
    Talking back.
    I. Title
    821'.914   PR6055.L/

    ISBN 0-436-14260-0

SUBSIDISED BY THE
Arts Council
OF GREAT BRITAIN

Printed in Great Britain by
Redwood Burn Limited
Trowbridge

Contents

359844

LIBRARY

MURRAY STATE UNIVERSITY

Talking to Horace

for John Milner

'I wonder what it's like at parties now?'

You'd still hear the familiar human row,
The sound of egos belling, face to face,
As if competing in a market-place
To sell themselves; but louder, for we walk
Or stand to drink, avoiding general talk —
A mob, you'd say, but in its Sabbath best.
I think you'd see that, though we'd not be dressed
In white like you, or uniformed by class.
Also, we 'smoke': a dried-up herb — not grass —
Held in a paper tube, burnt and breathed in,
To give a swooning sense of harmless sin.
Then, you'd see ladies drinking with us; and
No slaves (none of your coupling on demand).

'Sad loss!'

      Well!

             You'll be wondering, no doubt,
What Britons ('fierce to guests') could talk about.

'You're *British!*'

           Yes, and *sapiens* like you —
That's what two thousand years of thought can do.
Thus, at a northern house the other night
You were named twice. You're famous still all right,
Although your golden mean has disappeared
Like Croesus' gold . . . and Aristotle's beard.

Diffugere nives, but English thaws
Can't make our snow run off as fast as yours,
Even in March. So we were cold and late

Coming to toast a friend's new Doctorate.
(The belly, still, to honour a full head,
Calls in some friendly bellies to be fed.)
But first, with glass in hand, we talk: on pets,
Children, the cost of fluoride and vets,
Preoccupations of a family
That fret us all, now everyone is free;
Meanwhile our Doctor's younger son aged three's
Padding round barefoot, head above our knees:
We shuffle carefully, in case his nose
Catches some treasure guarded by our clothes;
The owner, by the fire, plays the male game
Of warm-your-breeches at the naked flame:
A separated viscountess; her man
And she would strike you as Italian —
I'd have said, 'Well-off artist,' by her looks.

Nice paintings, but no chance to see the books:
Oh, lucky painters, who without offence
Can scan your art at sociable events!

I met a 'farmer's wife' and asked her how
They farmed: she looked too frail to wield a plough . . .
They live by breeding Morgans (horses): she
Was born (like them) beyond the Atlantic Sea.
'I too' — but it was dinner-time, before
I could say 'crossed that Ocean — in the War.'

Eating by candle-light (but on a chair)
At tables forming three sides of a square —
Arrayed like Romans for attacking food —
I never thought of you, it was so good.
I forget all my pretty neighbours said,
But — would our menu please the gourmet dead?

'Go on!'

                We've found some new things, dear old-timer,
Since you concocted *Catius' eating primer:*

A fat red squashy vegetable, nice
Chopped up with lettuce, vinegar, oil and rice —
Love-apples — what your Sabine farmer calls
'Apples of gold' or 'Atalanta's balls';
Then, a gold berry, *Hesperidium*
(But found in India), whipped into a scum
With cream (from cows, not goats) and 'sugar' (honey
Would do), and gelatine (it wasn't runny);
But no more novel plants — you mustn't think
Us holus-bolus vegetarians: pink
Salted pork, sausage, cold domestic birds
(Do you recall the tastes, or just the words?)
And wine, still drunk (and drunk in every land,
Though one Arabian god has had it banned).

Dimmed by this meal we staggered up for hot
Drinks in the hallway. Some could dance; I, not.
The next thing I remember is a thin
Girl who'd begun a thesis on Dupin
And Labrunie, two Gauls well-known to Fame
(Though, like Ulysses, under a false name)
And even (she was hoping) to each other;
This was on top of being (twice) a mother.
I'd asked her what she did! — What do *I* 'do'?,
I thought (as fond of sleep and books as you).
Luckily then, to save me from self-blame,
A tall Pict (with a Jewish poet's name —
And not tattooed!), one of our best Horatians,
Walked up to us to talk about translations.

Glazed by now as an antique painting, I
Noticed my friends stood near to catch my eye:
Time to start driving home, through all that snow.
But, as I buttoned up my coat to go,
They turned me, almost hauled me back to greet
A smiling blonde face that I 'had to meet' —
I don't know why: she liked my poetry?
Something about an Open (Air?) Degree?

I liked her tomboy look — we'd met before?
(Had she a gold tooth in her lower jaw
Like mine?) Virginia? married to a man
(Like me) from an old Border reiving clan,
Now stuck in rural peace that even you'd
Find a bit deep — you'd call it solitude.

Stepping outside into the stream of night
That always seems the same, but isn't, quite —
For even heaven's not fixed, as you were told
(Your Sagittarius is bent and old),
I saw three white chairs standing by a round
White metal table on the snowy ground.
The seats, pushed back, looked dry and summery
Enough for timeless hospitality —
As if some guardian spirits had been there
Talking, and waiting to resume their care,
A moment such as our new Doctor paints:
Small man-made landscape, with invisible saints.

Were you there? Longing for your cup of blood
As Homer says?

    'You'll find out, if you're good.'

Talking to Bede

'You think historians must be keen to see
What followed their escape from history?
You think we can't find out? I'd rather hear
The earth described. Remind us of the Wear,
The creatures, plants and light where I began
To look around the domicile of man,
The home I only saw till I was seven.'

You miss the handiworks of God, in heaven?

'That's what we all must go without; so when
You die, bring news of nature, not of men.
None of us saw enough: we lived too much
In the small range of feelings, taste and touch.'

What, even you?

                    'You'd think not, but I still
Long for one walk across a field or hill.'

The Tunstall Hills, then, limestone — did you know
More than two hundred million years ago
They were a barrier reef, at the equator?

'I knew God made the world; I did think later —
As well as man's Last Judgement being soon.'

We still think that! . . . You've . . . heard about the moon?

'I know you . . . we . . . Man . . . Armstrong has been there,
Taking, as well as bait, a flask of air,
And whistled sweetly through the crystal spheres
We thought a solid mesh of ringing gears.
We got the moon wrong; but I told the tides
With some effect for sailors and their brides . . .'

Indeed you did. But how you told the tale
About the monks at sea without a sail!
Bringing down wood on rafts to Tynemouth, *they*
Were caught by wind and stream and borne away,
Till like a seabird swimming far from view
They hardly showed across the shifting blue.
Out rushed a squad of Brothers, with the Prior,
And knelt, and sent up prayers — like mortar fire!
I like your verse! — while the whole show was guyed
By local heathen from the South Shields side.
(For good men's fates give joy to reprobates!)
Among these Geordie rustics and their mates
Stood Cuthbert, still a boy, appalled to find
It isn't all that natural to be kind.
He tried to rouse Their Noble Savagery
To pray, and when they wouldn't, *bent his knee*
And pressed his face to earth. The wind backed east,
Or else turned turtle, for the future priest,
The rafts reached shore, and the embarrassed clods
Admitted Cuthbert's God outshone their gods.
        But surely the next tide, the evening breeze
Onshore, were not surprising prodigies
To you, but chance, coming out right for once.

'The eyes of sadness and of confidence
See the same world. You'll know whose eyes were sharp
Someday. Till then, keep looking, and don't carp.'

Forgive me, Bede. The old see more; the dead,
If anything, see more than can be said.
        Do you see Durham, where your leavings lie,
Translated from the Jarrow cemetery?
— 'Or rather, stolen, by a sacristan —
Aelfrid — a relic-crazy Westoe man — '
Who made you share a coffin — was that nice? —
With the shy saint whose *Life* you'd written twice.
        I went there from Pons Aelius upon Tyne
(Where Aelliots start to draw their family line?),
And saw, inside that one majestic room,

How blessed are the meek in Cuddy's tomb.
He's got two covers on his burial place:
One says, 'Ricardus Heswell', to his face;
The other, laid above it, back to back,
Is meant for us: CUTHBERTUS, gold on black.
They've left his pillow with him — Oswald's head —
But now you're honoured with a separate bed.
  I stood and thought of you, the Church's light,
Your only miracle that you could write
Here in the dark of Britain, stay-at-home
Doctor, Transhumbria's answer to Jerome,
Your undivided virtue ending on
The last notes of the Gospel of St. John:
'Even the world itself could not contain
The books that should be written. Aah . . . *Amen.'*
A life of ivory, in and out of books,
Leaving no record of your wit or looks —
The little teacher's jokes in your short course
On Writing Latin Right were never yours:
'Melissus said buttocks is feminine,
But Verrius recommends the masculine . . .'
'Tibiae: human shin-bones; later, flutes . . .'
'Riches is always plural — so is toots
(Darling — but only in the vocative) . . .'
'Bellus (lovely) has no comparative . . .'
And so on, tags I guess as old as Latin,
That sent a groan round classes Virgil sat in.
They take our feelings back to someone young
Trying the tastes of grammar on his tongue,
But not to you, I think. We can't see you
Or those you name — you didn't mean us to? —
Except: you wore your hair cut Peter's way;
In memory of the crown of thorns, you say.
Other men show us Caesar pleased at winning
A laurel crown because his hair was thinning,
Or Cleopatra's smile as Marcus took
His only catch, her kipper, off his hook,
Or, burning cakes he was supposed to cook,

The first translator of your *History* book.
You never give such details. But may I,
A disappointed customer, ask why?
I brood on how your Brothers used to make
The illuminations down by Jarrow Slake:
They drew with templates, compass and a rule —
Like pattern-lessons at an infant-school —
Or copied Bibles, inch by inch. Next door
You cut up Commentaries, and made more,
Wrote Christian elegiacs for relief,
Collected folk-tales with a saint-motif,
Learned from the authors on the library shelf
And turned into a scholar by yourself.
You never left Northumbria. But, Bede hinnie,
How could you take your geography from Pliny?

'Pax. Skinchies, Elia — Aelle — What's-your-name:
Forbear to judge. It's blasphemy to blame
The inhabitants of heaven, or of earth:
I wrote, like you, for all that I was worth.'

Since Dante put you in his *Paradise*
You don't need praise; and who could criticise
The writer who rose earliest to walk
About our glittering language, still all talk?

'Pity my native stuff is lost. God knows
I worked on that despised vernacular prose . . .'

Strange to compose without a lexicon!

'And spell the passing words, before they're gone,
Like Adam's animals, never seen before —
And maybe soon extinct, or heard no more.
    'Tell me about some animals, in fact.
Forget the Wear: thanks for your silent tact
About my birthplace and my monastery,
Despoiled by bookless raiders from the sea
And then by the original filth of man.
    'Show a consoling wonder — if you can.'

Oh Bede! Your churches of St Paul's and Peter's
Are kindly kept, with services and heaters.
Through the same windows Jarrow light still falls
On surpliced cantors in their choir stalls.
There's a Musaeum: people come for miles
To see torn straps, smashed glass, nails, broken tiles,
And not to touch, relics not even yours,
For holy curiosity, not for cures.

'Yes, yes, the leavings: when they come, they see
The horrible marks of human territory
All round, where no one wants to live. What monk
Prays in these deserts of industrious junk?'

I saw a wonder on a summer's day,
Bede: I was walking on the landward way
To Lindisfarne, and found the sort of place
That puts agnostics in a state of grace,
Two rivers north of Tyne. A little breeze;
Bright ripples in the underskirts of trees;
Among the flowers on the sandy shore
Hovered an insect overlooked before
In years of scarcely looking. It was stout,
Furry and pear-shaped, with the stalk held out
To drink its nectar from a moving cup —
Two wings, so not a bee. I looked it up:
Bombylius major L. — Linnaeus too
Had seen a bee-fly in his day. Did you?
I bet, like me you'd never heard of it.
　　Another first time, I watched cuckoo-spit
Nymphs blowing bubbles, and looked up at home
These things that lay their house in farts of foam:
Grown, they're the brown kind that shoot up like spray
From boots in heather or bare feet in hay:
Froghopper, typical homopteran.
　　For you, Bede, dry and fresh as that dry man
Whose book connects the stages of a creature
As if there were no miracles in nature,

I hope these views from pleasant earth can cross
The barriers of years and bodily loss,
And —

        'Yes. They reach me; almost with the smell
Of seasons I excluded from my cell . . .
Enough for now. I'll ask for a repeat
When it's your heavenly birthday.'

                      — If we meet.

'Benedictus benedicat!'

              And God bless
Your abbot Ceolfrith, patron of my Press,
And Benedict Biscop, your first abbot, who
Gathered the library that nourished you:
Tell them — they may be pleased — their fame's not large
Enough (like yours) to christen a garage,
But they're remembered where their scholar is:
You all gave names to Jarrow terraces.

John Elliot

(Auchendrain, January 29, 1844 — Glendhu, September 1928)

In the second decade of the railway age,
months after Henry James was born,
the same year as Verlaine,
my father's father arrived,
shouting across Loch Broom
while Mendelssohn's violin concerto
was being first performed.

A Gaelic childhood still,
on the mainland, with one book in it;
the Good Book was enough,
though above the barricades
the German Lazarus
worked upon more and more.
Oh grandfather, Scottish child . . .

As Germany was unified,
you earned your living on hills,
addict of peace and quiet
in Argyll, as Paris starved,
Verlaine eloped with his friend,
shot him and went to prison,
and taught in Lincolnshire.

In the year of *Bonheur* you married:
the line of sons began.
Verlaine wrote the poems I know so well,
the Lumières showed that train pull in,
Verlaine died, and Victoria died;
my father began to breathe
when you were fifty-seven.

Your daughter-in-law was born
with *The Ambassadors,* the first plane . . .
The Great War somehow began.
You and your orphaned wife from Nedd
paid two sons down; two more
fought at Gallipoli and in France;
my father helped with the Glencoul hay.

Henry James became British and died;
the war-to-end-wars came to an end;
my father went back to school,
and left the glens forever.
You watched him turn into a doctor
while Hitler was sentenced to rewrite *Mein Kampf*
and Rutherford transmuted matter.

Still never losing your temper,
you grew old in the long beard,
and died, before my parents met.
Years later, my father recognised your arm-bone
held out in the grave
at his mother's funeral:
I'd have seen you — if I'd gone.

Homeric Similes from my Autobiography

Part I

Like the fakir smiling to see the sky
as the warped lid scrapes open, and his sons
and daughters greet him ('Home on time for once!'),
and his wife waves the new best friend goodbye,
I . . .

As when the trumpets stop, you hear the quiet
conference of sparrows, and the captive feet
scuffing through files of neighbours down your street,
and one black mourner walks behind a chariot
looking at everything, and meets your eyes,
and passes, her pink palms chained to her thighs,
she . . .

Then, as on mountains when a shepherd looks
over pure world until he hears the knock
of wooden spoon on pot, and leads his flock
down through the dust to salesmen, thieves and cooks,
I . . .

Part II
Like the field-grey reoccupying rooms
where the earth-brown once sat, which everywhere
stink of danger (some far-off engineer
laughs in the desert at the thought of bombs)
and at the bar another language sings
the common song of people's underthings,
you and I . . .

But as the swift's granddaughter stops migrating
and hoop-las round a tower, and through the airs
bumpy with cooking cuts smooth arcs and spheres,
crying the hunt of insects up, and eating,
she . . .

Then longer than the pause when the cat's mother
enters and it runs up exchanging blows,
and they stand side by side but tail to nose
and seeing nothing each looks where the other
has walked from — till she turns to clean its fur
and it begins to feed, and blink, and purr,
we . . .

The Change

Unwanted days surround me,
as in a cafeteria:
congealed autumn with cold eyes,
ominous, and sloshy.

The delicious lashes and long tail
roll-calling round at dawn
bucking away or licking salty hands
have lost their personal taste:
these ladlefuls of Something
might have eaten Anything.

But further off the fauna of time still
wander uncaught,
twin days, Siamese weekends, timid mornings;
interested afternoons
catch whiffs of us thinking of them;
they hear us in the leaves beginning
our joint work on common months,
till now completely unstudied.

The water in our mouths runs again.

A Northern Morning

It rained from dawn. The fire died in the night.
I poured hot water on some foreign leaves;
I brought the fire to life. Comfort
spread from the kitchen like a taste of chocolate
through the head-waters of a body,
accompanied by that little-water-music.
The knotted veins of the old house tremble and carry
a louder burden: the audience joining in.

People are peaceful in a world so lavish
with the ingredients of life:
the world of breakfast easy as Tahiti.
But we must leave. Head down in my new coat
I dodge to the High Street conscious of my fellows
damp and sad in their vegetable fibres.
But by the bus-stop I look up: the spring trees
exult in the downpour, radiant, clean for hours:
This is the life! This is the only life!

Homines Sapientes

Walking to work like someone's dad,
We lick at history on the way
Through sunlight and a mile of moor,
And taste the crispy modern day,

Relishing the near touch of earth:
Our toes remind themselves they tread
On something living that can grow
Lying at home all day in bed.

Pedestrianly, we overtake
The neighbours in their traffic-jam.
Pleased with our free old-fashioned gait
We laugh: 'I walk; therefore I am.'

But then we see a horse laid out
Motionless, swollen, on one side,
One of the ponies from the fair
That cost you such a lot to ride.

Then we see — no — it isn't dead,
Just dozing; and beside it lies
A man, his back against its back.
An arm, a tail wave off the flies.

He sucks at grasses: 'He's at work
Already.' And with envious looks
We pass, to your illiterates
And to my multilingual books.

359844
LIBRARY
MURRAY STATE UNIVERSITY

Lunch-Break at the Hotspur Hotel

A sheet of glass, the whole front wall, lets in
pale cloud-reflected light on our faint grime.
The beer is clean. A strange electric lie
whispers the nunc bibendum of pub-time.
Curtains cut off all but the noblest heads
and tops of things.
                  A man back from the south
to die, mentions a birthday or a win
and buys us all a round. I have a pie.
Kirstie comes in, who works the Norway boat.
Pictures of married daughters. She makes beds
and tends the bar. Why don't I sail across? —
she will look after (and looks straight at) me.
I buy a round now, wondering if my balls
(tightening at the seam) would play the goat
among ship-smells and salty metal walls.
We kiss, searching the inner walls (applause)
for messages of life lost in the mouth,
for bumps and grinds on lower North-Sea bunks,
years grander than our own.
                  I leave, sadly,
and not as one who dares: as one who funks.

A Revelation

The white-haired man stands in his lonely job,
where I wash my hands. 'Had lots of sun?' I say,
'You're so brown' — healthy as a body-snob —
'Is it a Spanish tan?' (Had it away
on some blond beach where buttocks and the sand
compete to warm each pensionable hand?)

'No, this year we just went to the south coast.
I'll tell you something strange . . .' Then quietly
(white walls have ears? some bugger's listening post?):
'Down there it gets dark sooner. It must be
an hour — the sunset — earlier than here.
I wonder why that is. Isn't it queer?'

Wonder can be like joy. Since then, all day
my mind has turned to see the age-old view
he sees. Surely he knows . . . The Milky Way,
the miles of nothing we are spinning through
at an angle to the planetary floor . . .
'Strange,' I say slowly, opening the door.

Public Address

All behave quietly here.
The voices on the air
feel nothing: they are signs
for the hot listener to
thaw, like a frozen book.

*The building closes in
five* . . . means, for instance, *FREE!* —
or, if you prefer, *OUT!*

This is the dead word trick
(guess what the face is like
above those muted cords),
but it's sometimes followed
(they forget to switch off)
by private life, gratis.

The whole building listens,
sweating, to the rustle
of unmade conversation
(what will they take off next?).

Under the microscope
amoebas glide unheard,
a whisper of fluid;
here's our call, familiar
to the other species,
unknown to us: seconds
of shuffle, sentences
walking off for a piss,
half-words and hand-held jokes —
behind, to prove it's real,
the cosmos drizzling
like a rather shy clock.

Agonising to hear
life at metronome speed —
worse than hearing your self
as you sound. A relief
when some warm finger turns
our raw universe off.

John Eateth the Book

(page heading from the Breeches Bible at *Revelation* 10)

'John eateth the book.' I understand:
I see them daily copying their books
In a machine, imagine them at night
Stirring the powdery meal, with one slow hand,
Eager to eat the carbon and the light
So magically prepared — by other cooks.

'It shall be in thy mouth as sweet as honey,'
The angel said, but 'It shall make thy womb
Bitter.' The bloody vegetable ink
Brings in the aftertaste of work and money;
The Word itself glows in us, till we think
There is a goodness that may overcome.

I Know Thee Who Thou Art

Chilled in the dusty nearly level sun
Of March among the buildings, I decide
To ambush buses elsewhere; then, one comes.
(The urban gospel: 'Sod's Law will provide.')

I settle by a window, in the last
Place left where one can keep on being one.
The man behind me dithers in the aisle
Among averted eyes and sprawling bums,
Looking for friends. Because I got on there
I seem the less a stranger
                                    — till he sees
Poetry Nation glaring on my knees.

I hold it to my chest; and with a smile
Make room. It takes some courage to sit down:
He bravely does, but starts to rummage through
His plastic carriers, not to speak.

                                    His face
Is plump and spotty, stuck with bits of hair
That don't seem his. The sky's a brilliant blue,
As everyone, except a *Poet,* says —
So I sit speechless.

                    In my part of town,
I just grunt, 'I get off here,' and squeeze past.

Saul

When we have kidney Meyerbeer —
at home now; we have not been back —
I think of you, where I first tasted it,
dark and solitary in the restaurant.
'It must be five years — more?'

We reminisced no doubt: now I recall
(as I pick up deliciously stained rice)
a poem you had shown me, in Perugia,
about English trains heard far away at night;
the mystery of painting; your terse uncle,
original of Basil Seal, in Rome
recommending islands; our American friend,
Luigi, who would come to Bonn
for Beethoven's two hundredth Geburtstagsfest,
who taught us a cheap breakfast, of raw egg
and Marsala; your lithe little half-sisters
swimming at Cosa; Amanda! and their mother
English as wild flowers; your dark curly head
not ominous then over the shaded lunch.

Soon after my first kidney Meyerbeer
I heard from someone you were found, hanging,
in your London attic. Something unbearable
had taken away the taste of everything.

Years and years later, gathering the last grains
of this saddening but often-repeated meal,
I remember my room in the Via Antenori:
wakening there in the dark to flash after flash —
not lightning but a little glowing fly:
it floated round the walls, another life.

There is always something to be happy with?

Seeing You in a Documentary

People pass on the boring promenade
not looking round, until your face up there
closer and closer turns to the camera,
as if you knew, that grey uncertain day,
the sight of you would travel, miles and years,
with no forbidden writing and no stamp,
to where my disbelieving face, half here
after another crisis, turns and sees
its second wife dissolve before its eyes,
dark glasses brutally expressionless.

To My Son Aged Ten

The Sunday noises of TV next door
remind the old in their last home — and me —
of the tradition, a world of hymns:
a nation singing, recovering from a war,
lives growing up like plants to definite heights,
at a botanical speed: how we looked forward
to being grown-up! You, complete already,
lie back reading among the foreign colours
(the cotton carpet from Baghdad). And I:
every evening is different; will I ever
see you like this again? My ghost groans
adding here to the places it must haunt.
I weep behind my hand in sympathy.

House-Rules I: Reading

Among the white walls we read quietly.
The rugs beam up unnoticed.
We try not to read out the bits we like:

There you are swimming on your back in some dark lake
squinting with wet eyes at some friendly constellation
when this madman begins skimming out coloured stones.

The beautiful sofa of my cell
gets solitary, with you over there.
Life pours away, a whisky tap left on:

Here I am treading water out of sight of land
when up foams someone wearing nothing, in her hand
some bread and butter and the mermaids' local paper.

House-Rules II: Lights

Taking all armour off
taking off all protection
you come to me, carrying
like something delicate in a paper bag
yourself in your skin.

Air moves out of the way:
a bow wave must be coming
but I feel nothing,
until the warmth, the comfortable circles
of marriage, lie down
beside my open palm.
Strange permission, of nakedness together:
like being alone, not modest, uneventful
among the laws that cannot be repealed.
Lights off (our light); and reconvene
the interrupted lifetime of our bodies.

After, the aboriginal cold
creeps in under the clothes: Jack Frost
master of all
putting his finger on our brows and necks,
who will outlast even *Amoeba proteus*
now celebrating somewhere with his clone
his three thousand millionth birthday.

A Touch of Death

Strange fingers woke me, fumbling at my brow.
My rooms were near a roof. I thought: Somehow
Someone's got in. The cold hand hit my nose.
Naked between the freezing sheets, I froze.
Then . . . nothing happened. I became aware
Horribly slowly no one else was there:
Quite dark, but you could sense across the floor
The usual wooden quadrupeds, no more.
Was it a corpse's hand, put in my bed
By my best friend, who's studying the dead?
Surely he'd not do that . . . The arm felt grey,
Somehow, and yielding, in a foul soft way.
It didn't smell, though. Feeling worse, and colder,
I ran my left hand up it to the shoulder,
Expecting torn-out strings, a bulb of bone,
And wetness. Worst of all, it was my own —
I'd two right arms: one, warm beneath my head
And pillow, there; and this, cold, slack, and . . . dead?
I tried to touch the real one where I knew
It must be, but my fingers went straight through.
All the sensations of my arm lay there
In order, like a well-lit thoroughfare,
But not the arm. My soul is breaking free,
I thought: I'll lose the arm. I might lose me!
I grabbed the dead thing. It was powerless.
I rubbed the muscles, stroked and tried to press
The blood along, like air in a balloon,
But nothing made it feel. It would die soon,
If it weren't dead already. Then I thought:
If I could swing it round, it might get caught
As it goes through its image. Can you fit
Your arm back in the space that matches it?
The elbows fused together as they met,
The wrists and knuckles too — a perfect set.
And even when I moved them on, they stayed
United as they'd been since they were made.

I felt the rushing happiness of a boy
Who's found the key he needs to wind his toy.
I slept then, I suppose. I don't recall.

You'll keep this quiet, won't you? After all,
Who'd ever shake this hand — with which I write —
Knowing it died and met its ghost one night?

Allah Akbar: Winter: A.H. 1344

When Shiraz was Shiraz, Cairo was one of its suburbs
Persian proverb

Outside the city, *sahra:* miles of dust.
But you heard lions roaring: all night long
The dark blue lid was filled with this wrong noise.
'They don't have lions here! It can't be lions!'
An Indian circus . . . with the handsomest audience:
I sat amazed among the Ghashghai nomads.

December: in a taxi, with a pot,
I'd bring lunch home (the Garden of the Sheikh,
With exhibitions of the kinds of leaf) —
A twist of sumac dust, a yolk of egg
And yoghurt, rice, kabab, Islamic beer:
The unexpected happiness of meals . . .

Across the road (they say) the King of Kings
Drained off the blood that disagreed with him;
Around the corner someone generous
Gave goods away (just breaking someone else);
At our gate a beggar couple propped a child
Hired by the hour and drugged to look like death.

Going to work, I'd stop a taxi, shouting
'Literature', and if he shook his head, get in.
Wildly, as if he rode a horse, he'd drive me
To the Knowing-Place of Courtesies — House of Sin,
Said one (because the students never wore
Those long dark veils sprinkled with tiny flowers).

One day you told our servant I'd invited
Seven monkeys to dinner: 'Get a pound
Of sheep's ears.' O, to be a foreigner!
The week it rained I went one afternoon
To bargain at the *baazaar.* Dim and quiet;
I met a man who taught me how to play.

He sat me down and gave me *chai:* Was I
From Englistan? I lived in . . .? 'Bagh-e-Sheikh.'
Ah, I spoke Farsi. Yes, he had a fine
Kettle (a tinny thing) for ten tomans . . .
'Amrika-y nistam, vali Englis.'
Well, perhaps eight? 'I wanted a less fine . . .'

We spoke. His bearded face laughed into mine.
We drank another cup. More happiness
At sitting in the world exchanging words
(And goods) — the envy of all travellers,
Who, where the mountain road displays Shiraz,
Kneel in the dust in tears: Allah is great!

Recalling the Goddess: Spring: A.H. 1345

The statue of Shapur . . . at the mouth of a cave three miles
up the valley . . . climb of 600 feet . . . perpendicular, and I
stuck . . . Mr Hyde carved his name on it in 1821 . . . swim
in the river . . .

Robert Byron, The Road to Oxiana

'When I was at Beal . . . the one-armed bandits . . .'

'When I

was . . . took a taxi . . . tyres blew out three times . . .
kept a good lookout . . . bandits, the nurse said . . .
they were ten years younger — finally I gave up . . .
I thought I'd die . . . the cave . . . nothing to drink
but a bottle of warm vodka . . .'

When I went,

we got off where the old (Sassanian) road
angles down rocks to the plain of Kazerun.
The tea-house; the carved rock; a man pissed, squatting.
There, the fire-temples and the heat: I too
felt my age — L. was obsessed by it.

Among the orange-blossom streets we found
a hotel: and after eating, in the moonlight
saw some abandoned houses sudden as bomb-sites,
being sanded down by time. Smooth brown tiles
by the four beds in our room, instead of Bibles,
to touch your forehead on when bent to pray.
They slept with their faces under the quilt, feet bared.
(I dreamt of you — the act of population.)

In the morning, soft-boiled seed-of-hens, tea, bread.
Now I have learned to wipe my arse with water.
Cold and early, swinging into the truck,
with labourers — what can you say? — we smiled
at the handsome faces, ashamed of watches and travel.
A goat, kicked, under the seat. My back!
We passed the lines like bomb-holes in the desert

(a seventh of the able-bodied men
go down there every day, shepherds of water).

Skirting the mountains. Finally, Bishapur:
the road in a gully; red dust; a green tea-house;
man with a withered arm, proud of his glasses:
'My cigarette is silent. Have you light?'

We climbed to Shapur's castle. By the edge
of the red cliff in the soft stone we found
the place cut for him: he would face the dawn:
from below you'd have seen the crowd of hungry birds.
'It's really a bed' — L. got in — 'with a new twist
to getting out the wrong side in the morning.'
The clear air stretches out for miles, forever,
with the descendants of those birds still wheeling
unfed over their dry and tasty empire.
Goats and nomads all over the valley,
the overlapping kingdom that goes back
earlier than cities, the first kings of kings.

Below in stone Valerian kneels to Shapur.
When *he* died, he was stuffed and carried round.
Water is wearing the great relief away:
was it dangerous to walk barefoot down the stream?

Later, in the ruins (a criticised excavation)
we called on Anahita, goddess of water
who sings both day and night. We had watched in silence
the weavers in the tent; I had reached the cave;
I had seen the fallen statue — no warm vodka —
but plagued by a quotation from myself:
'not to be absent is the prayer of skin.'

The next day we went on, losing height, praying
at every turn in the deep dust, the driver
leading our chant, past strings of climbing camels
to the lovely wooden decors of the coast.

Genius for openings in walls. Verandahs.
Dhows. The forbidden island. Sinbad's gulf
and Milton's. A seal from Susa.

And flew back,
like M., but with no sharks under our arms,
to the family, the mulberry tree, the wall named Jim.

The Aegean: Summer: 493 B.C.

'. . . took easily the islands off the mainland, Chios and
Lesbos and Tenedos.'

Herodotus, *History* 6.31

There is something strange about so much blue.
And I cannot believe it has no edge:
it has the feel of this side of a cliff.
But it seems the fishermen say blue just goes on,
further and further. But it must run out
somewhere: so must the land. It does in islands,
so I suppose the mainland is an island.

Anyway we are here, conquering the world.
Travelling it would be enough for me:
but it also has to be kept. That's harder.
We have beaten their soldiers but these people
won't accept that — perhaps I wouldn't either —
so we have exercises like today's.

Daryush sent us to the island there —
I can see it from this table — peacefully
recovering, giving back the sun its heat —
to net and decimate the islanders.
This morning hand in hand and joining on
so as to cover the ground from coast to coast
— it was like a game; everyone was from Fars —
we walked across it letting them through the net
but quietly killing every tenth. The counting
was done by me for our section, and Farhad
killed them. I did the best I could to make it happen
so we killed not just men or not just women
but children too, to thin them equally,
so that each family would remember us,
but Farhad said he was tired of killing women —
and then we found a young one in a field.

Farhad said he couldn't — it would be like
spitting on food or pissing on the Fire.
He made her stay with him; took an old man
instead; but then, after a baby and a boy,
said he was too exhausted to go on.
We let him go — we could see the girl was lovely.

It's been a hard day. We are tired, and some
were seasick coming back.
                              They're calling me —
The scream was Farhad. As we should have thought
(but they had been trying to talk for hours and hours)
she killed him: bit his shame off, stuck a knife
under his naked ribs. I had to stop them
from killing her in turn. That is not right.

Perhaps it is her beauty and not justice
that made me save her, but I made them wait
for the Commander. Then when Daryush came
he just gave her to me: "He was your brother."

Mother, I can't. I don't know what to do.

A Farangi Broadens His Mind: Autumn: A.H. 1345

'He that travels in the Highlands may easily saturate his soul
with intelligence, if he will acquiesce in the first account.'
      Samuel Johnson, *Journey to the Western Isles of Scotland*

First the landscape was green, with pigeon towers,
like windmills without sails, hidden in trees
in the shallow vale (no river could be seen),
and the road ran among fields of bright young wheat.
Not a bad road, but soon it turned from black
to the same brown as everything in sight,
not boring brown but shades of buff and grey,
old battlefields of botany, rock, and drought:
not a desert — the driver doesn't pause
to pray for safety in this merely waterless place.

Occasional man on a camel in the distance.

After an hour of delicately scanning
these miles of absent lake in powder form
I had to explain myself across the aisle
in shouts, to a teacher who couldn't understand
travelling for pleasure. So we gave up that,
and I asked about the little roadside cairns:
what could these pyramids of twenty stones
signify? He was full of explanations:
They put them up to mark the road. 'But, please,
excuse me, we can see the road already.'
*It's for the winter, when because of rain
the road's a river.* 'But can't they see the river?'
The snow conceals it all. 'The stones too, no?
And still the road being lower' (using hands)
'than what it goes through shows itself far better
than a few stones.'
                  Then (as I'd long been hoping)
we passed a man kneeling in the great plain
to make a cairn, his folded coat beside him.

'Look, what's he doing?' *Who? I did not see.*
In the evening light I couldn't make him see
the dusty dwindling peasant.
                              Far from home
at nightfall people heap up stones for nothing.

Then through the window, as he stared at me,
I saw two people praying with the sun
lengthening shadows down the orange slope,
their coats beside them: and they faced two cairns.

'Look, it's a guide for praying towards Mecca!'
Again he missed them. And polite as ever,
The Holy City is another way
and nobody needed stones to pray toward it —
disgraceful thought! We didn't speak again:
outsiders are not serious human beings.
How could they understand or behave well?
No wonder they have to travel to learn wisdom.

Getting off, I bowed, my hand across my heart.
Hastily he did too. *And God protect.*

My Country, 'Tis of Thee (1940-45)

in memory of Esther M. King

O my America, you are so full,
I'm always having to repack you. Like
A mother, wanting space inside myself,
I shove my pre-war Katzenjammer Kids
Under my first American bed (late '40),
And linger over one of me, eleven,
In a baseball tree, batting the apples out,
And ('The Financial Lesson') pedalling home
Along Lake Worth at dusk, a Chinese fall
Cascading in one hand: a wealthy man
Stops me and makes me sell it for a profit.

Delicious amateur America,
Favourite museum, where so many things
Bear the wrong labels or are unexplained,
And everything's earlier than the atom bomb —
I've something to donate. Let's throw away
'Sitting in Palm Beach in the Messerschmitt
In the spring of 1941' — will that
Clear out enough? — or this, the whitewashed room
In the empty house, with dead leaves on the floor
And the receiver dangling, with Chicago
Dead at the other end (some crook had lived here)?

I'll keep the cottonmouths (shot with a B.B. gun);
The yellow-zeppelin kumquats and tummaytoes;
Baudelaire, Elinor Wylie, Frank L. Baum
(All in the attic); L.S.M.F.T.! —
O my America! This time I've brought
Not some caricature from your enemies,
Not a line of verse, or tale of tasteless bread
And policy, but a little mended finger:
Thanks to a rubber-band and safety-pin
(*Kleinert's Traction*, from Tennessee), my hands,
Hands anywhere, can applaud again; or fight.

The Latitudes of Home

Here I read Biggles; in this chair, *Ulysses;*
Here I watched sperm wriggle across a slide
Slower and slower as their element dried;
In this back corridor I gave secret kisses
To tins of sweet milk, other people's blisses;
Ironed on this table; underneath it tried
To find the pleasure grown-ups used to hide;
And here faced east for several thousand pisses.

Meanwhile my father earned the means of life
At this thin desk; my mother was his wife;
The cost of living rose each dreamy year
Till now: his surgeon, gratis, lifts a knife
And starts to cut him; and I think with fear
Till now I never wrote a poem here.

The Last British Battle

for Pauline Dower

Your uncle, the hard-walking historian,
Described the place (trying to please his father):
Drummossie Moor lay quiet, as in shock;
To the south, beyond the neolithic circle,
Some navvies built a viaduct; and north
Across the firth, within an outstretched arm,
The gentle Highland mountains turned their back
On Highlanders being butchered through this heather,
The haze of distance in the blur of death.

My Stewart ancestor was there, that April,
Killing his man perhaps, that personal way;
Wounded, escaped the field and hid alone
Some nights; then, giving up his former life,
Made for the Northern Lights, the rocky farm,
The seaweed harvest, and a Gaelic wife —
A happier ending than his bonnie prince
Would have in Rome, prime victim of Drambuie,
Unable to give up the old pretence.

At Saxtead Green

So we climbed the broad steps into the mill.
It was quiet, with an insecticidal smell,
not old-fashioned at all, unlike the levers,
and loops of thong, and wooden chutes and bags
which spread their fainter fumes among oiled cogs
and grinding wheels under new wooden covers.

The two of us tried to see how the power
flowed down these catching circles through the floor
into the stone, while the boys had to climb
and pull at bars and ropes, and worry us
with cries and sounds of falling. So you made peace,
waived understanding, and left with one of them.

Then Willy pulled a string, and the whole mill
began to shake, obeying some unheard call
with coupled forces, which it seemed would smash
the precious antique parts — *we'll both be killed!* —
the runaway air-turned-iron uncontrolled
threw round the creaking works in a thunderous rush.

Somehow I kept bare hands from intervening
and dragged us safely out into the evening,
where on a bench the guardian still sat
stroking his dog, and you admiringly
watched the sails turn: it was the wind, not Willy,
rising a little, that had caused all that.

I almost broke their toy, I almost had
thousands to pay, one of us might be dead . . .
still churned inside me. Knowing it was not
an accident but a coincidence
didn't much help: *so the mistaken sense*
could throw me into gear without a thought . . .

Horrible when the deep machine takes over:-
puking on terra firma, the land-lover
helpless because a face has come or gone.
You had to drive us home, so I was free
to look back at the great sails emptily
turning. Better worked idly than not run.

On Holiday

Shut in their legendary summer
as real as mine
with golden light common to both
the boys run

quiet as night-bound lives that zoos
shift onto days.
Seeming to avoid our eyes, to hear
no urban voice,

they ignore the pale inquisitive grown-ups
trapped and fretting
through the same hours, on the far side
of something —

thoughts like shop-windows standing between
us and our ease,
or like a surface holding back
fish from flies,

till, going down to the North Tyne
for a starry piss,
I find I'm not discreetly drizzling
into the grass

but pattering on great leaves like rhubarb:
what I shatter
under the dark near-African trees
doubled in water

is not the composure of a scene
and a man,
but silence, the one shield at night.
Frightened, I hurry in.

Ingredients of a Sleepless Night in Wales

Lager from Wrecsam; heard over the phone
— words posted directly down the ear —
of a friend's death by drowning (the North Sea
with sun on it last Monday); wading back
to bed through fields of dew (not whispering now)
among hills ennobled by the sun's last rays;
delivering David's message from the pub
like a speech (about calves) to a kitchen full of folk;
tea; conversation (two women more than men);
and trying to tell by noses who is whose;
hearing (from bed) their parting stories — how
farmers can laugh, how much they can allude to! —
and then the noises of the immature night:
a shot at half-past twelve, a little later
repeated jerks at a fence (somebody wounded?
Morse? should I get up?), the unsleepy bed
in the next room, with healthy little children
visiting their healthy parents in the hot dark.

But how well you feel in the morning — light unpacks
the daily present; swallows on the wire
practise turning to face the other way;
skin in the sheets still able to imagine
everything suddenly wrenched out in the sea.

After Heavenfield

Trailing our battle-perfumes, we fall down
to the undusted stream, and stick our blades
into the muscling water. The cold flow
bears off our weariness as well. We hear
the rush of elements, and look round again:
'God, what a cut!' 'There's something in your beard.'
And thinking of our families and the wives
of those we buried on the hill, we dip
our helmets for a drink, and throw the rest
at friends, liquid that sparkles in the air
and glows on backs. We shout: We won! We won!
and bare-arsed in the sun, we share the bread
on crumbling stones, and brush the flies away,
and eat in silence, as the morning goes.

Trying to Read Outdoors

The seeds of rose-bay willow-herb float down,
swirling in silence on the streams of air
above the noisy river. Now and then
a leaf is softly turned, turned back again,
the silky scholarship of summer.

Still more the insects, golden after lunch,
prick out the turbulence. Some draw bright lines
across a shadow; most, in fuzzy schools,
drift on a current, intermingling files,
or hit the water, race their engines,

and vanish, struggling, eastwards. I am old
compared with them and what I lean against,
thinking about the endless lapse of fluid;
but their kind got here first. We share the world
a little, equally entranced

by sunlight: a biography of rain
is someone else's, and my rowan tree,
air-sick or earth-sick, but outliving man,
holds up its prehistoric feast again —
to the dark birds of the next century.

Alexandrines for Livy

In Livy's wonderful history of the city
From its foundation, there's just the triangular ball
Out in the water, and the leg, its famous boil
Pulsating by the knee. Everywhere else is misty,

At first: behind thick cloud Aeschylus sweats and thumbs
His worn-out sword; a nameless Indian invents chess;
Three Aztec prisoners can't sleep; early forms of us
Lose their virginity, their axes, querns and combs.

But here, already focused, round the consuls' tent
Plebeian faces, deafened in their helmets, lean
To the great argument: will their centurion,
Named Marcus Flavoleius, call a strike, and end

The future empire? We are stirred; but they don't know
There are a hundred volumes someone's got to fill.
For Christ's sake, on the horizon Greece is visible.
Won't there be panning shots of elephants and snow?

Won't there be Livy? Sitting here and looking down
We see his book hauled up in jerks through layers of time
Like Simeon Stylites' lunch, and feel the column
Of history trembling now — as it has always done.

Epistle to an Alien

Here in my kitchen, conducted through a continuous sunshine
by the grandfather clock, with cadenzas from an old fridge,
I am picking an argument, just for the sake of music,
out of the night behind tongues, our black artesian cortex,
with the unanswerable dead, the language-hunter and trainer,
Auden, who put his head in the mouths of dictionaries so well
we were no longer amazed, and some had forgotten to read him.

Dear poet, dearer now you are silent as Caesar and Stalin
than when your atoms made sense and your molecules
                                        autographed fly-leaves,
why (when you wrote with cousinly sorrow of daily disasters
suffered by creatures who cultivated your skin) did you think so
ill of the Insects? You wrote, *What Saint made a friend of a*
                                        roach or
preached to an ant-hill? It happens there was such a moment;
                                        each evening
in a Greek jail one man in solitary rolled up his shirt-sleeves
for his three thirsty friends, mosquitoes, who would remember
at a concurrence of light and dust and odours of cooking
George Mangakis, land among hairs, and drink from the runway.
They gave him what friends give: times and reasons for meeting,
bar-lines and rests, a structure, occasional hints of a theme-song.
When he was moved to another cell, he missed them. They
                                        couldn't
find him.

        One instance can, and this does, falsify theories:
breaks in the filament. But the lighting-threads in a poem
carry just part of its current; they lie like yesterday's dinner
seen through the dome of a jellyfish, hazily being digested.
Feeling jumps over the gaps. Your poem (irregular ending
and all) has what we ask of poems here in the cosmos:
something we want to learn, a game to play over and over,
flaws in the rules being only a Muse-given pause for refreshments.

In the disordered atmospherics of nowhere it must seem
quite dissolved though, like everything made by our thought
                                        and our bodies
(even replacements we so humanly, vainly, engender) —
like yourself, Auden, now, who seeing the too-unemphatic
face of truth realise *what we must never become.*

Straightening Out Virgil

> *caeruleos implexae crinibus anguis*
> *Eumenides*
>> *Georgics* IV. 482-3

As Orpheus sang, the very halls of Hell
And inmost sculleries yielded to the spell;
And the Eumenides stood stock-still there,
*Those dark blue snakes tight-*knotted in *their hair.*

    The Saxons were destroying Roman Britain
    As our best manuscript of this was written:
    In rustic capitals IMPLEXAE *twined*
    Coils among tresses for the reader's mind.
    One day an ancient hand, perhaps the paw
    Of Apronianus (consul 494,
    The owner), in a brainwave made it better
    Than Virgil had, by taking out one letter —
    IMPEXAE: Furies that you mesmerise
    Must get their *uncombed* serpents in their eyes.

    Another (Rustic is as Rustic does)
    Conceived it was the same — INNEXAE — as
    In *Aeneid* VI: 'Great! The Eumenides,
    In hair*nets* made of sea-green vipers, freeze.'
    And all the learned men of Charlemagne
    Nod, 'Yes — except, AMPLEXAE: they *contain*
    Their hypnotising wig of snakes with . . . hair.'

Ixion's wheel stops in the windless air,
Cerberus' muzzles gape and gape and gape;
And going back he's *managed to escape*
With his Eurydice returned again,
When . . .

A Warning to Wordsworth: or, the Lay-Detector Rampant

... the intensity of emotion expressed in the 'Lucy poems'
occurs elsewhere in Wordsworth's poetry of the period only
in those poems involving Dorothy and, therefore ... she
becomes the leading candidate for the original of Lucy.
This conclusion leads logically ... (etc. etc. etc.)

Donald H. Reiman *T.L.S.* Nov. 1, 1974

Dear William, watch it: he can read your pulse,
but Wasserman-tests all your waters first —
'Tis three foot long, two wide' is something else,
and mirrored mountains make him fear the worst.

'Proteus rising' (shades of urethritis!)
leads on to London's sweetly gliding pee,
but Venice has the best claim to excite us:
'She must espouse the everlasting Sea.'

Can he declare you treated as a wife
the unvisited City (ooh! its Grand Canal!)?
'The dreary intercourse of daily life'
meant no-holds-barred to a Romantic gal?

And what went on in Davy Jones's locker
when she encountered her drowned sailor-brother?
Something no doubt not quite according to Cocker-
mouth standards of a kiss or bit of other.

Be warned then, though perhaps it doesn't matter
if hygroscopic poets are abused
or glotterotic critics merely flatter:
soon all are far more deeply interfused.

Reply to a Painter

'Our stuff may not be pretty,
but at least we've got a Muse.'
Choerilus of Iasus (Letter to Apelles, c.325 B.C.)

An art of peaceful objects! You make things
From bits of world, possessions that we keep
In rooms, or graves, useful like wedding-rings,
Symbols to guard, and polish, dust, or sweep.
But poems aren't the paper, cloth, stone, wood.
They're found between the senses and the pulse,
In dark pink catchment areas where blood
Washes the words of men and animals.
They replicate: the copies are as new.
We carry them invisibly. They lie
Unmelted in the mouth through all we do,
A hundred light as one; and when we die,
They sweeten, incorrupt, some younger head:
The immortal public property of the dead.

Finishing Off a Book

Open-mouthed, the poems look up like fish
from the carpet where they lie, scattered,
hungry for juicy readers.

I remember a valley where distributed sheep
all turned and stared at me:
My God! a guest without a tie!

How will I round them up? A sheep-dog-fish?
A liquid whistle stirs nothing
but dust in my extra-marital room.

I assert myself: I'll sort you!
Finally I do, parting families,
twins, friends of the class of '71.

And grow cold to them: schools, flocks,
something to sell. Something to give:
something to give away?

Dedications! tracks of a doubled life,
names that inspire creative questions
between the sheets, in the pocket-money queue!

And books have names: not Rex, not Daisy —
*Airs of Return, Heat Transfer in Packed Beds,
The Skin is the Best Part, Contentions* . . .

Kiss the man goodbye.

Acknowledgements

I am grateful to the editors or literary editors of the following journals, in which some of these poems first appeared: *Encounter, PN Review, Thames Poetry, Iron, London Magazine, Times Literary Supplement, Poetry London, The New Statesman,* and to the BBC Radio 3 monthly programme *Poetry Now;* also to Michael Schmidt, editor of *Ten English Poets* (Carcanet, 1976), and the editors of the Arts Council's annual *New Poetry 2, 3* and *4.* 'Recalling the Goddess' first appeared in 1978 as a pamphlet printed and published by Libanus Press, Hermitage, Berkshire. 'The Aegean' is reprinted (with thanks) from my first book *Contentions* (Ceolfrith Press, 1977) and from *Poetry Introduction 4* (Faber, 1978).
I should also like to express gratitude to my employer, the University of Newcastle upon Tyne, for a six-month leave of absence in 1979, and to my forbearing colleagues in the University Library. I gratefully acknowledge the assistance of the Arts Council of Great Britain at that period.

Note: The opening stanza of 'John Elliot' alludes to the family tradition that my grandfather was born while Mendelssohn's violin concerto was receiving its first performance. After writing the poem I discovered that the tradition, fifty or sixty years old, is based on a mistake — probably encountered in George Dubourg's history of the violin (5th edition, 1878), which I have not seen.

DATE DUE

DEMCO 38-297